Also in the
Klukwan History Book Series
by
Lani Hotch, *Saantaas'*

Kaaya Haayi Hít

Klehini Naaxein

Klukwan Founding Fathers' Story

Klukwan Healing Robe

Klukwan's Legacy of Warriors

Our Life is Close by Our Food

Tsirku Héeni Naaxein

Uncle Albert's Ku.éex'

Lani Hotch, *Saantaas'*

Jilḵaat Héeni Naaxein (Chilkat River Woven Robe)

A Klukwan History Book Series story of the weaving of the Chilkat River Woven Robe and the creative process that went into making it. Book one of the Three River Robe series.

This book was written by Lani Hotch, *Saantaas'*.

It was edited by Liz Heywood and Dan Henry.
Photos were provided by Lani Hotch.

Text and photos were compiled by staff of the
Klukwan Community and School Library
for the
Klukwan History Book Series Project.

Funding for this project was made possible by a grant from the Institute of Museum and Library Services. The Institute of Museum and Library Services is the primary source of federal support for the nation's 123,000 libraries and 17,500 museums. Through grant making, policy development, and research, IMLS helps communities and individuals thrive through broad public access to knowledge, cultural heritage, and lifelong learning.

Jilḵaat Héeni Naaxein

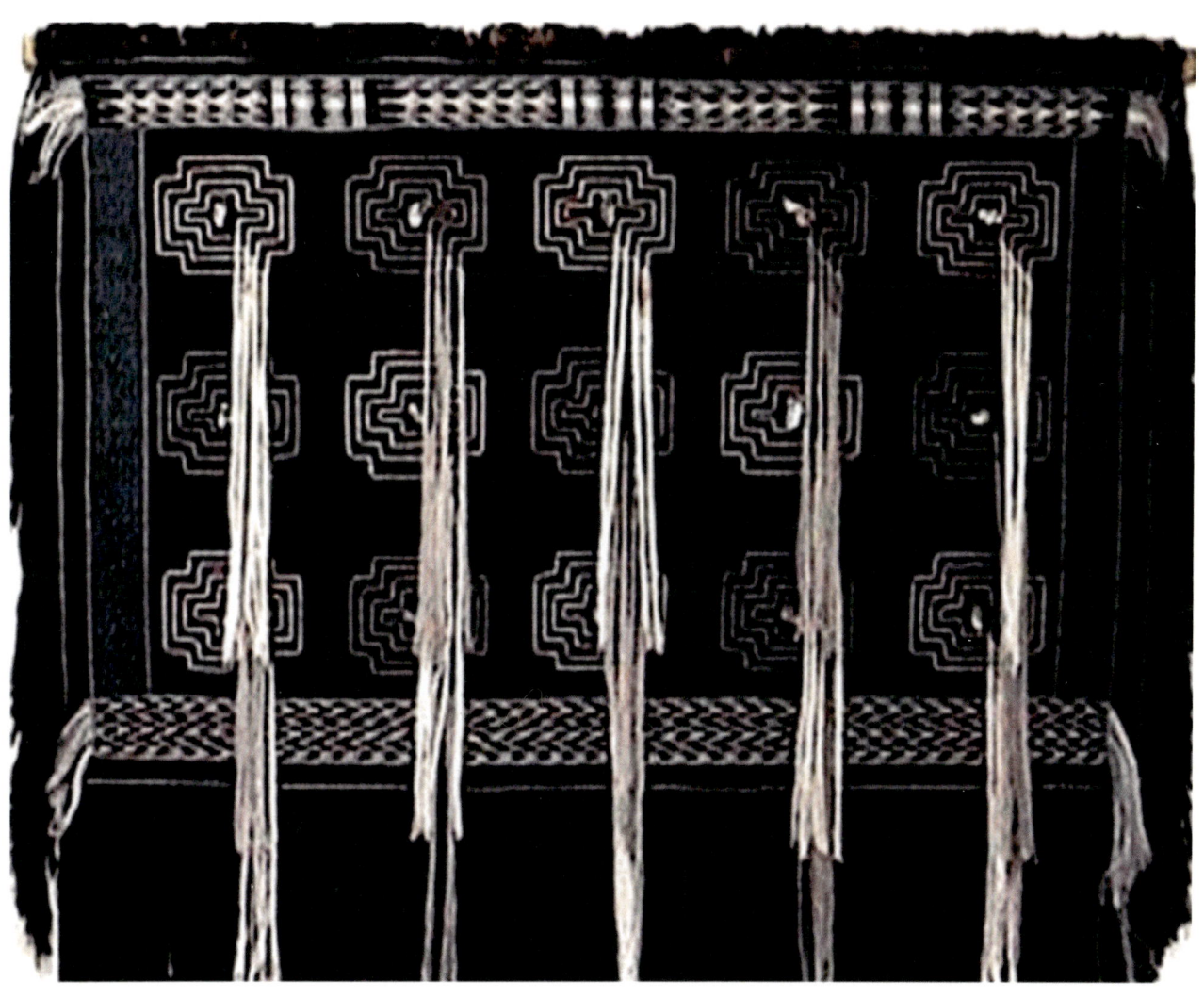

About the Three River Robe Series of Books

Klukwan is situated on the confluence of three rivers, the Chilkat, the Klehini, and the Tsirku. My original intention was only to weave the Chilkat River Robe, but after completing the Chilkat River Robe I decided to create weavings of the other two rivers since they are major contributors to the Chilkat and they converge right at the site of our little village. Each of the three weavings has a different focus, yet there are some design elements that are repeated — the "backbone of the salmon" design is found in the Chilkat River Robe and the Klehini River Robe, and the "tree reflections" pattern is found in both the Klehini and Tsirku River Robes. Each weaving has its own story and I share those stories in this trio of books. I believe that by sharing the stories of the weavings I am helping people to fully appreciate both the weavings and the creative process that went into weaving them.

Jilkaat Héeni Naaxein (Chilkat River Woven Robe)

What do you do when you first meet someone? Most people exchange names and ask "Where are you from?" My question to you is: Why do we want to know where others call home? Think about that for a while. Perhaps it is because the environment leaves an imprint on your personality. Where you come from, or where you choose to live, has a large part in defining who you are as a person.

I was born in *Tlákw Aan* (Klukwan, literally "Eternal Village") and have lived most of my life next to the *Jilḵaat Héeni* (Chilkat River), so the river has left an indelible mark upon me. The *Jilḵaat Héeni* is not

noisy, but in the quiet of warm summer evenings I can hear the water flowing. In the *táakw* (winter) the water level of the river drops drastically because of the freezing cold weather, and then the eagles gather here in very large numbers -- up to four thousand! Some days I look out to so much fog that a wall of gray blocks all views. Other times the river flats and trees are covered with snow and the braided streams of the Tsirku cut across the Chilkat River flats, just before they

enter the Chilkat, creating blue and black veins that make lovely patterns against the white snow. It is breathtaking in its beauty. One of the benefits of living in Klukwan is that I often get to see birds and animals on the river flats -- *xóots* (brown bears), *kichyaat* (terns), and the occasional *láx'* (heron) in the summer and *gooch* (wolves), *dzísk'w* (moose), *gáaxw* (ducks), *kageet* (loons), and *gúḵl'* (swans) in the winter. The *héeni* (river) is ever changing and yet, constant. Its constancy is one of the things in my life that helps keep me grounded.

In *haa ḵusteeyi* (our way of life) people are not thought of as separate individuals but as members of a family, clan and community. Our formal introductions include our *Tlingit* name, our *naa* (moiety), clan name, *hít* (house) group, and our father's and grandparents' clans. Here's my introduction: "Saantaas' *yoo ḵat duwasáakw, Lingit xeinax* (They call me Saantaas' in *Tlingit*). Lani Hotch *yoo ḵat duwasáakw*, English *xeinax* (They call me Lani Hotch in English). "*Ch'áak' Naa ḵa Kaagwaantaan ḵat sitee* (I am of the Eagle Moiety and *Kaagwaantaan* Clan). *Gaanaxtéidi yadi áyá ḵat* (I am a child of the *Gaanaxtéidi* Clan) *ḵa* (and) *Gooch Hít dáx áyá* (I come from the Wolf House).

Gaanax̱téidi dachxán (I am a grandchild of the *Gaanax̱téidi*) *ka Jilkaat Kwaan dáx̱ áyá* (and come from the Chilkat People). This is a very formal way of introducing one's self in the Tlingit tradition. This introduction does more than let people know your name; it helps the people you meet know how you fit into the larger contexts of family, clan, and community and, in the process, strengthens one's own sense of belonging. This formal introduction also reinforces the Tlingit values of honoring family and community.

The designs on our tribal regalia also indicate who we are. Clan crest figures such as *ch'áak'* (eagles), *gooch* or *kéet* (killer whales) are typically worn on our regalia. If you are familiar with Tlingit or Pacific Northwest Coast formline designs, crest figures on regalia will reveal the clan and moiety of the wearer. You will likely know their hometown, too. This instant recognition is similar to how United States citizens associate Olympic athletes with the United States when they carry the American flag. Sometimes clan crests depict landforms like a mountain or a point of land, or even a large rock instead of an animal or bird. In my case, I wear the *Jilkaat Héeni Naaxein* to show where I come from--- Klukwan, the "Eternal Village" that is situated on the *Jilx̱aat Héeni*.

The top border of the *Jilḵaat Héeni Naaxein* shows the "backbone of the salmon" design. One of the first things I learned about making *at x'éeshi*, (dryfish strips) was to take out the backbone. When I was taught this skill by *aḵ léelk'w* (my grandmother, also means grandfather) Jennie Warren and my Uncle Albert, I knew I was off because Uncle stood behind me making these sounds like "*ts-agh!*" He showed a lot of restraint because I know he really wanted to take that *lítaa* (knife) out of my hand. I was leaving way too much meat on the backbone, which was considered wasteful and taboo with Uncle Albert and Grandma. Grandma dealt with the problem by hanging the backbones on the branches of a dogwood bush that grew nearby. "For the birds," she said.

Now, when I cut *ḵáat* (fish) or *at x'éeshi*, I save all the backbones of the *ḵáat* and boil them to create fish stock, which I pressure-process in quart jars and use for making *útlḵi* (boiled salmon) in the *táakw* (winter).

The side borders of the *Jilkaat Héeni Naaxein are* called the "hooligan dip net" pattern. The Tlingit name for hooligan is *saak*. They are small, oily fish that return to the *Jilkaat Héeni* in the early *táakw eetí* (spring). *Saak* bring the first annual feast of *taakw eetí* from our bountiful *héeni*. The traditional *saak* dip nets were triangular, thus the concentric triangular form of this design element. Now people use aluminum dip nets or throw nets, but in the old days the nets were handmade from alder saplings. They were quite heavy compared to the ones used today so it took a strong person to use them. *Saak* are eaten fresh, dried or smoked, and if taken in large enough quantity, can be used to make *saak eex* (hooligan oil).

The bottom border of the *Jilḵaat Héeni Naaxein* depicts the river or rippling water. The waters of the *Jilḵaat Héeni* are glacially fed and are gray with silt in the summer and clear in the *táakw* months. For that reason I mixed the colors of white, blue and grey in the *Jilḵaat Héeni* design which isn't really a pattern but more of a free-form random weaving. The randomness of this design reflects the ever-changing nature of the *Jilḵaat Héeni*.

The center field of the *Jilḵaat Héeni Naaxein* has a modified cross pattern that is referred to as the *Yéil koowu* or "Raven's Tail" pattern. The "Raven's Tail" pattern, in this weaving, represents *Haa Shagéinya* (Our Creator/ Protecting Spirit). In the middle of these patterns are bits of abalone shell. The iridescent shells have a silver-blue cast that remind us of x̱áat (salmon).

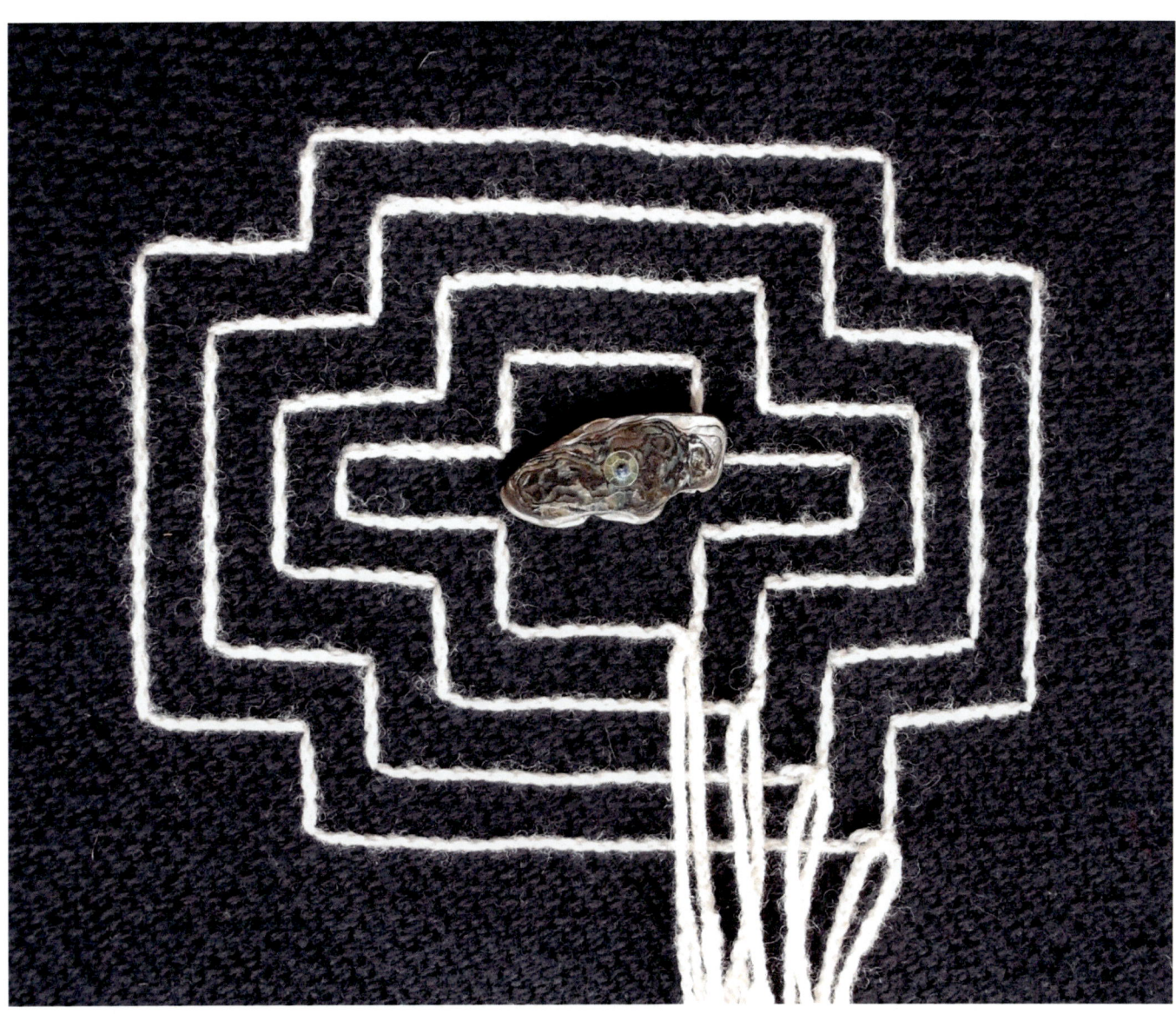

Five species of _xáat_ run up the _Jilkaat Héeni_: _T'a_ (King Salmon or Chinook), _Gaat_ (Sockeye or Red Salmon), _Téel'_ (Dog Salmon or Chum), _L'ook_ (Coho or Silver Salmon) and _Cháas'_ (Humpies or Pink Salmon). Within the weaving tradition whatever additions are put into the concentric patterns in the center field are considered "treasures" so I placed the abalone pieces to represent the five species of _xáat_ that are truly the treasures of the _Jilkaat Héeni_.

The *Jilḵaat Héeni* is so much a part of me that I sometimes tell people "the Chilkat River flows through my veins." If you think about it, it is true in a very real sense because I eat *ẖáat* and *saak* from that *héeni* and I drink from a spring that feeds the *Jilḵaat Héeni*, and whatever a person eats or drinks enters their blood stream. In a symbolic sense, the *Jilḵaat Héeni* is an essential part of me and the place I choose to call home. It is for these reasons that I wear the *Jilḵaat Héeni Naaxein* ----- to show the world who I am, and where I come from. *Yei, áwé* (That's the way it is).

Lani Hotch is a Klukwan resident who lives a traditional subsistence lifestyle, putting up traditional foods such as salmon, berries, wild game, and foods grown from her garden. Lani was born in Klukwan and has lived there most of her life. She and her husband, Jones Hotch, Jr., whose Tlingit name is *Naatl'*, have been married for over 31 years at the time of this writing (2014) and have three grown children. Creating traditional textile arts such as Chilkat and Ravenstail weaving and felt appliqué button blankets are a passion with Lani. She has woven six major pieces herself thus far, and has taken the lead on three group weaving projects.

Ms. Hotch was also instrumental in developing the Klukwan Traditional Knowledge Camp – providing grant writing and administrative support to the building projects as well as coordinating the activities of the camp.

Writing is not Lani's first love but she has written this series of books out of a desire to share this important history with the generations to come. Lani is a member of the *Kaagwaantaan* clan, Wolf House (*Gooch Hít*) and Eagle (*Ch'áak'*) moiety in Klukwan.

Glossary

at x̲'éeshi – dryfish strips

ax̲ léekl'w – my grandmother, also means grandfather

ch'áak' – eagle

cháas' – humpies or pink salmon

dzísk'w – moose

eex̲ – oil

Gaanax̲téidi – Raven Clan

G̲aat – Sockeye or Red Salmon

g̲áaxw – ducks

gooch – wolves

Gooch Hít – Wolf House

gúk̲l' – swans

haa k̲usteeyi – our way of life

Haa Shag̲éinya – Our Creator / Protecting Spirit

héeni - river

hít – house

Jilk̲aat Héeni – Chilkat River

Kaagwaantaan – Eagle Clan

kageet – loons

kéet – killer whales

kichyaat – terns

láx' – crane

lítaa – knife

L'ook – Coho or Silver Salmon

naa – moiety

saak – hooligan

T'a – King Salmon or Chinook

táakw – winter

táakw eetí – spring

Téel' – Dog Salmon or Chum

Tlákw Aan – Klukwan, Eternal Village

útlxi – boiled salmon

xáat – fish

xóots – brown bear

Yei áwé – that's the way it is

Yéil koowu – Raven's Tail

Tlákw Aan
"Eternal Village"

Made in the USA
San Bernardino, CA
14 June 2016

Photo by Ron Horn

Photo by Ron Horn

Also in the

Klukwan History Book Series

by

Lani Hotch, *Saantaas'*

Jilḵaat Héeni Naaxein

Kaaya Haayi Hít

Klehini Naaxein

Klukwan Healing Robe

Klukwan's Legacy of Warriors

Our Life is Close by Our Food

Tsirku Héeni Naaxein

Uncle Albert's Ḵu.éex'

Lani Hotch, *Saantaas'*

Klukwan Founding Fathers' Story

A Klukwan History Book Series title
that tells how Klukwan was founded by a
Gaanaxtéidi man and his four nephews

This book was written by Lani Hotch, *Saantaas'*.

It was edited by Liz Heywood and Dan Henry.

Photos were provided by Ron Horn and Lani Hotch.

Text and photos were compiled by staff of the
Klukwan Community and School Library
for the
Klukwan History Book Series Project.

Funding for this project was made possible by a grant from the
Institute of Museum and Library Services. The Institute of Museum and
Library Services is the primary source of federal support for the
nation's 123,000 libraries and 17,500 museums. Through grant making,
policy development, and research, IMLS helps communities and
individuals thrive through broad public access to knowledge, cultural
heritage, and lifelong learning.

Klukwan Founding Fathers' Story and Totem

Foreword:

Since our stories are passed through generations and elders rarely reference numbers of years, nobody knows exactly when these events took place. Although the basic events of this story are true to the oral tradition, I have taken artistic license to embellish the events with details taken from my own imagination and life experience. I have used some *Gaanaxtéidi* (name for Klukwan Raven Clan) names for the nephews but you should know that their real names, as well as their uncle's name, were not remembered by the elder who shared this story with me. If you would like to hear this story as I heard it you can find it at the Klukwan School/Community Library or the Haines Borough Public Library under the title Klukwan Elders Oral History Project-George and Margaret Stevens. Although George indicates that our founding fathers came from Sitka, other elders say they came from a community on or near *Taan* - Prince of Wales Island - and it seems that the latter version is more likely since there are still *Gaanaxádi* clan members in some Prince of Wales communities. Because of this evidence I have changed their origin to Prince of Wales Island rather than Sitka. I must add, however, that there are a lot of families who live in Klukwan who trace their ancestry to Sitka. Many of the *Gaanaxtéidi* men had married *Kaagwaantaan* (Eagle Clan) women from Sitka, and it could be that the founding fathers did as well.

Klukwan Founding Fathers' Story

See.éi was a rather plump young woman with one long braid that went down her back. She usually worked hard like her sisters-in-law and other women in the clan house. Although she was from a high caste family she was not afraid of laboring. However, on this particular morning she was desperate to see Raven's Breath, the man who had captured her heart in her youth. When her sisters-in-law asked her to go with them to pick *k'áach'* (red ribbon seaweed) she complained of an injured ankle.

"My ankle hurts. I can't even stand on it. Why don't you women go ahead without me. I will pick my *k'áach'* on the next low tide." Her husband, *Yéilkaa* (Raven Man), shot a disapproving glance her way as he left the clan house with his fishing partner. When they were gone *See.éi* stretched out on her sleeping furs and noticed *Gaakaltín*, an old woman of her husband's clan, weaving a basket on the other side of the firepit. *Gaakaltín* felt *See.éi's* eyes on her and she glanced in her direction. *Gaakaltín* narrowed her eyes and muttered, "The *k'áach'* may not wait for you. Those who like to sleep go hungry."

See.éi didn't care what the old woman thought. It was none of her business anyway. After her sisters-in-law had been gone for a while, *See.éi* slipped out the door while *Gaakaltín* was not looking. *See.éi* walked to the fishing site of the man she admired so much, Raven's Breath. He was a handsome man, strong and kind. Raven's Breath was never impatient like her husband, *Yéilkaa*, and she wished he was hers. *Yéilkaa*, however, was of a higher caste and her mother insisted that she marry him instead. It was the custom in those days for mothers to arrange marriages for their offspring with someone of similar social standing from an opposite clan.

While Raven's Breath was working on his fishing gear *See.éi* hid in the bushes to observe him. He stopped working for a few minutes to watch the *sháal* (fish trap) he had rigged up in the stream. There were already two *x̲áat* (salmon) in the *sháal* but he waited for more. He was deep in thought as *See.éi* snuck up behind him and tugged on the back of his trousers. He spun around and saw that it was her.

University of Washington Libraries, Special Collections, NA#3093

"Aagh, you startled me. I didn't expect you today," Raven's Breath murmured.

"I got out of picking *k̲'áach'*," *See.éi* responded. "I told your sisters that my ankle was hurting so I could come to see you. I haven't seen you for days and I couldn't wait any longer. I'm sorry. Do you want me to leave?"

"No, no, of course not. But are you sure it is okay for you to be here today?"

"Yes, the other women have all gone to pick *k̲'áach'* and my husband is out fishing for *cháatl* (halibut). They will all be gone for hours," *See.éi* explained. "Do you want me to help you with the *x̲áat*?"

"Well, I really do need to try and catch some *x̲áat* but I think I could take a little break," Raven's Breath replied. "I have been missing you, too, but I don't want to cause any trouble with your husband or family."

"Let's not worry about that now," *See.éi* whispered as she embraced him from behind. Raven's Breath put aside his fishing gear to hold her close for a moment. Then he pulled his *sháal* gates out of the water so if any _x̲áat_ were caught in his absence they would not go to waste.

He stashed the gates of the _sháal_ into some bushes and turned to take _See.éi_ by the hand. He continued to hold her by the hand and led her into the forest.

Meanwhile, the women on the beach south of the village were busy gathering _k'áach'._ Stands Like a Man had her basket nearly full,

Photo by Heather Lende

Photo by Lani Hotch

and Rushing Water had already started spreading her _k̲'áach'_ out on the upper beach to dry. Rides Whales was rinsing hers in a deep tide pool while Ancient Threads rinsed hers in a stream that flowed down the beach.

"I like my _k̲'áach'_ a little less salty," said Ancient Threads.

"Aagh, you're taking all the flavor out," Rides Whales exclaimed.

"_Aaa_ (Yes), you should rinse yours in the salt water like me. That way it keeps the flavor of the sea," Stands Like a Man chimed in.

Not missing Stands Like a Man's insinuation that her method was superior, Ancient Threads replied, "There is still plenty of salt and flavor after I rinse it in fresh water, and I don't like it to have too much salt. It makes me too thirsty." With that explanation the others left Ancient Threads to rinse her _k̲'áach'_ in the fresh water.

When all were finished with their work they gathered up their baskets. They strapped the largest baskets to their backs and carried smaller ones in their arms.   The women walked in silence through the woods on the well-worn path back to the village. Rushing Water went ahead while Stands Like a Man lagged behind.

Ancient Threads and Rides Whales walked companionably and while they were still some distance from the village Ancient Threads said, "Stop! I hear something." Rides Whales stood still and listened.

"What could it be?" Rides Whales whispered.

"I think the sound is coming from that direction," Rides Whales said as she began pushing through the alder brush with Ancient Threads right behind her. They came to a clearing just in time to see Raven's Breath and *See.éi* escaping into the brush on the other side of the clearing. Rides Whales and Ancient Threads looked at one another, eyes wide and mouths hanging open.

"What is it?" Stands Like a Man queried as she finally caught up with them.

"I don't know if we should say. . ." Rides Whales said slowly, looking to Ancient Threads for direction.

"I think *See.éi's* husband will want to know," Ancient Threads stated. "I am not sure that I want to tell him, though."

"Maybe we should tell our _kaa sháade háni_ (clan leader/spokesperson). He will know what to do," Rides Whales suggested.

"That's a good idea," Ancient Threads said, and Stands Like a Man nodded in agreement.

When they got back to the clan house they took care of their _k'áach'_ by laying it out on some makeshift tables made of planks and tree branches. When they finished, Rides Whales and Ancient Threads went to find the _kaa sháade háni_. The men were just coming in from fishing and they saw *Sháade háni* carrying a couple of smaller *cháatl* on a rope.

"Fresh boiled *cháatl* for dinner," he said with a big grin. "I hope you both are hungry."

"Yes, we are hungry," said Ancient Threads, "but we have an urgent matter to discuss with you."

"Can we talk over there?" Rides Whales gestured toward the *atx'aan hídi* (smokehouse).

Photo by Lani Hotch

"We saw something today that means trouble," Rides Whales started.

"Trouble for everyone," Ancient Threads added.

"What could that be?" *Sháade háni* asked, a shadow settling on his face.

"When we were coming back from the south beach with our *k'áach'* we heard some noise in the woods and we went to investigate and saw *See.éi* and Raven's Breath together," Rides Whales blurted.

"They tried to hide but we saw them," Ancient Threads added.

Sháade háni said nothing but just looked at them. The implications of this information broke through as his face blanched slightly. His features were frozen in place. Finally he spoke.

"This does mean trouble. *See.éi*'s husband is not going to take it well. Raven's Breath will have to leave the village. It is the only way that peace can be restored. I am not sure what we can do about *See.éi*. She comes from a high caste family. Her clan will not receive this news well and will place all the blame on Raven's Breath. That is why he will have to be banished," *Sháade háni* concluded.

Ancient Threads nodded her head solemnly and Rides Whales looked like she was about to cry.

"Don't say anything to anyone," *Sháade háni* said. "I will deal with this at the proper time."

"We will tell Stands Like a Man that *Sháade háni* instructed us not to say anything about what we saw," Rides Whales said as she began walking toward her *tláak'w* (maternal aunt), Stands Like a Man.

"Here, let me help you with those baskets, *Tláak'w*. They must be heavy for you," Rides Whales said as she lifted the basket full of *k'áach'* out of Stands Like a Man's Hands. Quickly, Rides Whales whispered that Stands Like a Man should keep quiet about what they saw.

"Under *Sháade háni*'s orders," Rides Whales added.

The afternoon proceeded uneventfully as the women turned their *k'áach'* in the late *taakw eetí* (spring) *gagaan* (sun) and the men stoked *x'aan* (fire) in their *atx'aan hídi* where the *cháatl* hung to dry. As the daylight hours waned, the scent of *cháatl* soup wafted in the cooler air of nightfall as women prepared the evening meal. Clan members gathered around the x'aan pit and filled their wooden bowls with the steaming chowder. After they were close to finishing their meal *Sháade háni* stood and pounded his staff on the floor.

"*Haa, haa, haa, haa, haa, haa,*" he chanted loudly. "*Haa, haa, haa, haa, haa, haa,*" he repeated again as he pounded the floor. He did this four times before he stopped to speak. "I have something very heavy to talk about this evening."

All was quiet in the clan house. Even the babies were hushed. An unruly log snapped in the firepit and the log sparked and the flames leaped, momentarily lighting *Sháade háni's* face. His deep-set eyes seemed even more recessed, and had lost their sheen. His was the face of grief.

"Somebody has broken the law of our people and he must be dealt with," he said as he looked around the room. His eyes rested on Raven's Breath. "Raven's Breath has been found with another man's wife. He must be banished from the clan house and the village. The woman he was with belongs to another, and she comes from an important family. It is not our place to deal with the woman I speak of. If we were to do anything to her it would evoke the wrath of her clan upon us. Therefore we must do what we can to smooth things over here. Raven's Breath will have to leave, and the woman, whose name I will not mention, will stay here with her husband."

As *Sháade háni* spoke, Raven's Breath sat frozen, jaw clenched. *See.éi* shrunk from sight and *Yéilkaa's* face was purple while the tendons on his neck protruded and pulsed. He had recently sensed something between *See.éi* and Raven's Breath, but didn't want to believe it. Now his eyes were blackened pits. He rose and pushed toward Raven's Breath, but two clansmen pulled him back. Raven's Breath stood—eyes riveted on the angry husband—and backed away. His two eldest nephews, *Aanlahaash* and *Kakáayi*, grabbed Raven's Breath's arms and led him out the door; his two younger nephews, *Skooyéil* and Raven's Wing, followed behind. They consoled their *káak* (maternal uncle) once they

Photo by Ron Horn

In this carving the four nephews are pictured above Ravens Breath.

got out the door and away from the clan house. Then *Skooyéil* and Raven's Wing offered to gather his belongings for him and *Kakáayi* said that he would gather some food. *Aanlahaash*, the eldest, stayed with him so they could talk.

"*Káak*, where will you go?"

"I don't know, *Aanlahaash*. I will try to find a new place where nobody lives. All these rules and people troubles are too much for me," Raven's Breath growled. "I will find a place where I can live at peace and not have to worry about anybody else but myself."

"No, *Káak*," *Aanlahaash* objected, "I will go with you. You will not be by yourself."

Just then, *Kakáayi* returned with a bentwood box full of *at x'éeshí* (dryfish), several bladder bags full of water, and two woven baskets, one filled with *laak'ásk* (black seaweed) and the other stuffed with dried *k'áach'*.

"I will go, too," *Kakáayi* interjected. "We can take the *yaakw* (canoe) we finished last summer. The clan will have to make another to replace it."

Raven's Breath nodded his approval and they all walked toward the *yaakw* with the things *Kakáayi* had brought. By that time, Raven's Wing and *Skooyéil* had returned with more of Raven's Breath's belongings--- clothing and gear for hunting and fishing.

"That's all we could grab, *Káak*," *Skooyéil* apologized. "Everyone was staring at us, and I thought *Yéilkaa* was going to come at us."

"Gook (Go ahead)! Put it in the *yaakw*, then go back by your *tláa* (mother) and *tláak'w*. Tell your *tláak'w* that her sons are going with me."

"But *Káak*, we should go with you, too," *Skooyéil* protested. "If you leave without us who will teach us how to hunt and fish and all the other things we need to know?"

"I don't know, nephews, I don't think your *tláa* will want you to leave her," Raven's Breath said gently. The young men looked into his face eagerly until he relented.

"Okay, but you two are going to have to pull your own weight. It will not be an easy life. One of you must go back inside the clan house and tell your *tláa* and *tláak'w* that you are all coming with me. I don't want them to worry or think that you were victims of any retaliation from *Yéilkaa* or *See.éi's* clan.

"Okay, *Káak*. I can go back in and tell them," *Skooyéil* offered. *Skooyéil* left the group at the *yaakw* and returned before they hardly knew he had left.

"*Haa tláa ka haa tláak'w* (our mother and our maternal auntie)," *Skookyéil* announced, "are sad to see us go but they said it would be better for you to have us with you. They said we must all work

Photo by Ron Horn

together and take care of each other."

"Well, nephews, if you are sure you all want to do this, then let's do it," Raven's Breath said. "*Aanlahaash*, you best get some of that dried *cháatl* out of the *atx'aan hídi* before we go. I don't think there is enough food here for four of us. I guess we can always stop some place and fish or hunt." When *Aanlahaash* returned with the dried *cháatl* they finished loading the *yaakw* and shoved off. They paddled out to sea with the light of the nearly full *dís* (moon) to guide them.

"We should try to get as far away from the village as we can just in case *See.éi's* husband or warriors from her clan try to follow us," Raven's Breath said to his four nephews. They nodded and paddled on in silence. Not once did the nephews complain or question Raven's Breath's judgment as he kept them paddling through the night. Eventually dawn broke. They were miles away from *Taan*, the island from which Raven's Breath was banished. The morning air was cool on their faces and a light mist hung over the water.

"Let's pull into that cove over there and rest for a while," Raven's Breath said as he cupped his hand over his eyes to shield them from the morning *gagaan*. The *gagaan* had just crested the jagged, snow-covered peaks to the east and its brilliance blinded them.

Photo by Lani Hotch

The nephews turned the bow of their *yaakw* toward the west, away from the glare of the *gagaan*, and paddled toward the cove on the western side of the channel. *Aanlahaash* and *Kakáayi* jumped out of the *yaakw* as soon as they heard it contact the beach. The rounded stones on this beach were no threat to the bottom of the *yaakw* so they dragged it ashore. Enough so that the remainder of the group didn't have to get their feet wet.

"*Aa-agh*," said *Skooyéil* as he stepped out of the *yaakw*. "It feels good to stand on solid ground."

"*Aaa* (yes)," agreed Raven's Wing, stretching his arms over his head. "My arms are tired of paddling, too. It will be good to rest for a little while."

"It won't be for too long," Raven's Breath said. "We can sleep for a little while, just until *gagaan* gets directly behind us," added Raven's Breath as he pointed to the south. "Then we must shove off again. We will head north. I believe that somewhere in the north we will find a good land, where nobody has any prior claims. A place where we can make our own rules and there is plenty of food right around us so we won't have to work too hard."

It was obvious that Raven's Breath had been putting considerable thought into what type of place he was looking for.

"That sounds good, *Káak*," *Aanlahaash* said as he pulled some dried *cháatl* out of one of the baskets. "How 'bout you be the *kaa sháade háni* of our own clan.

"I have been thinking about that, too," Raven's Breath replied. "We will call ourselves the *Gaanaxtéidi*, because we have come out from the *Gaanaxádi* clan."

"I like the sound of that. *Gaa-nax-téi-di*," *Skooyéil* pronounced the new clan name slowly as if he were savoring the taste of each syllable.

"I like the sound of it, too, but can we save some of this talk for later?" *Kakáayi* butted in. "I would like to sleep right now. I am so tired my head feels like it is gonna drop off." With that *Kakáayi* took his coat, bundled it together for a pillow and laid his head gently down, right there on a grassy slope just above the beach.

"That looks like a good idea," *Aanlahaash* said, grabbing a soft leather pouch to use for his pillow. Soon the four nephews and their uncle were all stretched out on the grass, fast asleep. They woke precisely at noon with *gagaan* directly south of them. It was as if someone set an alarm clock, though none of them had such a device, nor had they even heard of such a thing. What roused them was the internal alarm clock that *Haa Shagéinya* (Our Creator) gives each person. You tell yourself when you want to awake and your subconscious mind, which has a direct connection to *Haa Shagéinya*, will wake you at the precise time you desired.

"Time for me to water the bushes," Raven's Breath announced as he headed for a stand of trees. The four nephews followed their uncle's lead, though less modestly urinating on the beach before loading up. Their uncle reappeared from the small stand of trees and stopped at a small freshwater stream to wash his hands and fill his water pouch. After filling his pouch he scooped some water in his hands and rubbed it over his face. "Let's see how far we can get by nightfall. If the *dís* hasn't lost too much light we may be able to make it a little further after *gagaan* has gone down. We will just have to wait and see how it looks at dusk." The uncle and his four nephews set off again. *Aanlahaash* began to sing one of the *yaakw* songs and that helped them to establish a rhythm and get all their paddles in sync with one another. "*Wei-----, Wei----, Wee-ee- yaa hei---, Wei---, Wei----, Wee-ee yaa hei----*" *Aanlahaash* sang. Then Raven's Wing and *Skooyéil* joined in. They sang for a little while, and once the rhythm was well established they stopped. The only sound was the paddles breaking through the water. Occasionally a *kéidladi* (seagull) or a *yéil* (raven) called amongst the tall spruce on the water's edge. Once the *yaakw* got too close to a flock of scoters and they raised a racket as they began to take flight - all that fuss only to land a short distance away again.

Photo by Ron Horn

The group paddled on for hours, then pulled ashore again as *gagaan* began to set. The clear sky began to turn orange as a few wispy clouds balanced on the mountaintops took on a purple hue. The colors of the setting *gagaan* intensified as it began to sink behind the western range, then faded to grey before darkness fell.

Aanlahaash gathered driftwood for a <u>x</u>'áan and *Skooyéil* joined in. Raven's Wing and <u>K</u>akáayi were looking for food in the pouches while Raven's Breath filled the water bags from a nearby stream. The <u>x</u>'aan crackled and <u>K</u>akáayi skewered some *at x'éeshi* (dried fish) for roasting. The open <u>x</u>'aan heated the oils in the <u>xáat</u>, releasing an alluring fragrance. The uncle and his nephews stuffed the crispy, hot *at x'éeshi* into their mouths.

Raven's Breath made *s'ikshaldéen* (Labrador tea) by dropping heated stones into a small bentwood cooking box. *<u>K</u>akáayi* gathered some *yaana.éit* (cow parsnip) to round off the meal and *Aanlahaash* produced a small lidded box full of *tsaa ee<u>x</u>* (seal oil) for dipping. By the time they finished their meal the *dís* was high but only at half strength. Raven's Breath looked up at the *dís*, contemplating whether they should press on or not. The nephews watched him, waiting for some indication as to what he wanted to do.

Photo by Ron Horn

"Well, I think we will be okay if we stay close to shore. We will move on. We should make it to Tenakee by morning. I know some people who live in that area. I am sorry I didn't have time to prepare gifts to bring with me. Hopefully there will be no trouble when we get there." With that they shoved off.

The *yaakw* cut through the waters of the Inside Passage---waterways that divide the many islands of Southeast Alaska. The tide was ebbing and there was little wind so the water was calm. They paddled quietly, everyone watching for rocks close to the shore. The night seemed to go on forever so when Raven's Breath saw a sheltered cove around a point of land he told his nephews they would spend the remainder of the night there. They pulled the *yaakw* onto the sandy beach up past the high tide line. The crew each found their own space to bed down, none too far from the *yaakw*.

When they awoke in the morning they were surprised to smell smoke and when they looked down the channel they saw a fire on a stretch of beach. They could also see the steam of the warm springs rising from the pool near the fire. (This location is known as Tenakee Springs. Although it was not the site of a Tlingit village, it was a location the Tlingits in that area frequently used.)

"I knew we were getting close but I didn't realize we were that close," Raven's Breath announced. "We better get cleaned up and mix up some paint for our faces before we arrive."

The nephews bathed themselves in the salt water and afterward *Aanlahaash* brought out his small box of *tsaa eex̱*. Raven's Wing made a small *x̱'aan*. After it had burned long enough to produce some good coals Raven's Wing took a piece of wood from the *x̱'aan*, grabbing an end that had not been burned. He dipped the charred branch in a tide pool to take the heat out of it. Then he scraped the charred wood with his bone knife and mixed the black soot with *tsaa eex̱* to make some paint. Raven's Breath watched him and said "*Yakéi* (That's good)," and he used his forefinger to make black stripes across the cheeks of his nephews. He dipped his finger in the makeshift paint for each stripe he painted.

When all the nephews were painted Raven's Breath asked *Aanlahaash* to help him. *Aanlahaash* streaked Raven's Breath's cheeks with three vertical stripes and his chin with three vertical stripes. Afterward they loaded their belongings into the *yaakw*. Before they boarded, Raven's Breath paused. He looked at each of his nephews and spoke sternly.

"I don't want us to make any trouble with these people. We will let them know we are just passing through. We don't need to tell them why. I will just tell them we are going on an exploration journey just so I can teach you nephews some things about hunting and protocols for meeting with other people. It is not likely that they will question that. We will sing a song out on the water before we land so that they can hear us before they see us. That way they will know we aren't trying to sneak up on them. *Yee sikóo gé*?" (Do you all know it?)

"*Aaa*," the nephews responded together.

"*Yen ǵé yeewunéi ldakatyeehan?*" (Are you all ready?)

"*Aaa*," the nephews responded again in one voice.

"*Gook dei,*" (Let's go,) ordered their uncle. They lifted the *yaakw*, carried it back down to the water, and jumped in. *Aanlahaash* stayed in the water to give the *yaakw* a shove until he was satisfied that it would float clear with all of them in it.

It wasn't long before they were directly in front of the group camping on the beach with the warm springs.

"*Aaa---haa----hee---yei---, Aaa hei hee yei---, oo--- oo--- oo---, Aa---haa--- hee---- yei, oo---oo--- oo---,*" the group sang as they drummed the sides of their yaakw. They continued with their singing until they saw a group of men approach them on the beach.

"*Adoo sa wéi ldakatyeeháan?*" (Who are all of you?) The head clansman called out from the beach.

"*Taan goo dax,*" (We come from Sealion – literally, but refers to what is known as Prince of Wales Island today) Raven's Breath answered.

"What is your purpose in coming here?" The head clansman inquired.

"We are just passing by on our way north," replied Raven's Breath.

"What takes you north?"

"I am taking my nephews on a journey so I can teach them all that they need to know," Raven's Breath replied.

"Come ashore," the head clansman commanded, and the group behind him began singing and drumming a song of invitation.

"*Haa---hei haa, hei haa, hei haa, haa----hei haa---hei haa---*," the group on shore sang and drummed in welcome as the *káak* and his four nephews paddled to shore. When they reached the shore Raven's Wing jumped off and began to drag the *yaakw* up onto the beach. A few of the men gave him a hand.

The *kaa sháade háni* of the group motioned for Raven's Breath and his nephews to follow him up to their campfire. The visitors were motioned toward the *x'aan* where a few women had prepared a meal. There was a bentwood cooking box near the *x'aan* and one of the women was using some wooden tongs to drop glowing hot rocks into the cooking box. As this was done the scent of the *útxli* (boiled fish) was released into the air. When the group sat down the other woman offered them some hot tea in cups of tightly woven spruce roots.

Photo by the Strong Family

Photo by the Strong Family

"*Gunalcheesh kunax* (Thank you very much)," the visitors responded to the generosity of their hosts.

"*Aaa*," the woman responded quietly and nodded.

The group visited with each other for the entire morning, eating the *útxli* and exchanging stories of hunts and close encounters with *xóots* (brown bear). When *gagaan* was high Raven's Breath apologized to their hosts for their need to leave so soon.

"Forgive us please, we have a long journey ahead of us and we should be off. We don't want to get caught in a storm or anything," he said as his eyes scanned the sky for threatening clouds. The *kaa sháade háni* of their host group looked up as well and pointed to the south.

"Looks like there may be some trouble brewing there," he said. "You may be able to stay ahead of it today but you may have to hold over for a day or so once it catches up with you."

"We will see if we can stay ahead of it," Raven's Breath chuckled. "I will give these nephews of mine no rest until we find a good place to hold over." With that said the group gave thanks once again and offered a last salutation as they pulled away with their paddles.

The uncle and his nephews spoke amongst themselves about their experience with their recent hosts ---- laughing at the remembrance of the *kaa sháade háni's* story about his encounter with a *xóots*. Evidently he had been hunting *guwakaan* (deer) with another companion and they had stopped at a good patch of *kanat'á* (blueberries).

Photo by Ron Horn

The _kaa sháade háni_ and his hunting companion talked while they ate their _kanat'á_.   The _kaa sháade háni_ did not realize it but his companion had moved some distance away while he continued with his conversation. The man could hear his companion on the other side of the _kanat'á_ patch and once in a while his companion would reply with a grunt. Finally, when he had his fill of _kanat'á_ and came around the patch to see if his companion was ready to move on, he came face to face with a _xóots_.   The man yelled and the _xóots_ bellowed in response. The _kaa sháade háni's_ companion heard the commotion and came rushing over, whereupon the _xóots_ turned and disappeared into the brush. The _káak_ and his nephews laughed at the thought of the _kaa sháade háni_ talking and the _xóots_ responding with his grunts.

"The _xóots_ do understand _Tlingits_ (humans)," _Káak_ explained. "Should you ever have such a close encounter with a _xóots_ you have to tell him you are not going to take all the _kanat'á_, you are only getting enough for yourself and your family. He won't bother you then."

The nephews thought this was funny and laughed but their _káak_ admonished them again.

"I am not joking with you. They really do understand. My _léelkw_ (grandparents) told me that _xóots_ is our _káani_ (brother-in-law). So we need to respect him."

That settled the nephews. The chatter stopped and the group once again fell into a near silent rhythm with only the sound of the waves and their paddles rippling the water. Occasionally, they heard a _kéidladi_ or two. Sometimes a _tsaa_ (harbor seal) would surface near their _yaakw_ and watch them from a distance. This morning they had some marine visitors.

"Look at that," _Skooyéil_ pointed excitedly on the left. About two _yaakw_ lengths away were a group of six _yáay_ (whales) swimming together. The _yáay_ came alongside the _yaakw_, their backs glistening as they would momentarily surface before submerging. One _yáay_ came so close that _Skooyéil_ was able to run his fingers down its back as it crested next to him.

"_Hoo hoo hoo_," laughed _Skooyéil_, his eyes twinkling as their _yaakw_ heaved in the water. "That was close!"

The *yáay* moved much more quickly than the *yaakw* even though the nephews tried hard to keep up with them. They followed the general direction the *yáay* took and then the group settled back into their rhythm once again. Without really discussing the event, they all felt that the *yáay's* interaction with them meant good fortune. The elders always instructed the young people to pay attention to the animals, birds, water, trees and so forth because they will communicate with us and teach us what we need to know. Raven's Breath was remembering what his *káak*, who had long since passed away, had told him in this regard. Raven's Breath was considering what the *yáay* were trying to tell them.

"I think they are showing us which direction to take," Raven's Breath announced to his nephews.

No sooner had he made the announcement in regard to the *yáay* when a *yéil* landed on the bow of the *yaakw*. It sat there for a good part of the day as if it were a figurehead. As the night settled once again the crew pulled the *yaakw* into a small cove and the *yéil* cawed and flew to a nearby rock as they reached the shore. "I think we are far enough away now so we don't need to paddle through the night. We will settle here until morning."

Photo by Lani Hotch

The announcement secretly pleased the nephews, though none said anything about it. Raven's Breath knew they were happy, however, because he could see they all had a certain jauntiness to their steps as they pulled the *yaakw* ashore and set up camp for the evening.

The group slept soundly and started the morning feeling refreshed. The nephews woke to a crackling _x'aan_ as their _káak_ had started morning tea, had dug some clams, and was steaming them for breakfast.

"_Ax eet yaan uwahaa, kunax_ (I am very hungry)," _Skooyéil_ said as he looked inside the bentwood cooking pot at the steaming clams. They were cooked with _laak'ásk_ which made them even more appealing. "I think I will go and look for some _kóox_ (Chocolate Lily/rice) along the beach over there."

Aanlahaash pointed to a meadow where the _kóox_ with the starchy, rice-like root would be likely to grow. It would complement the clams and seaweed. The others watched _Anlahaash_ as he walked toward the grassy area.

"It would be good to have some _kóox_, but I don't know if I can wait," _Kakáayi_ said as he eyed the clam-seaweed mixture.

"Go ahead and eat if you want," Raven's Breath gestured toward the wooden cooking pot. "If he finds some _kóox_, we can save it for later." The nephews sitting around the _x'aan_ began to dig in.

"_Aaah, linúkts, Káak_ (It tastes sweet, Uncle)," Raven's Wing said as he licked a little of the _laak'ásk_ from the corner of his mouth.

"_Yei awé_ (That's right)," _Kakáayi_ agreed.

"_Aaa, yéi nateech_ (Yes, It doesn't get any better than this)," said _Skooyéil_ as he scooped a little more clams and seaweed into his wooden bowl.

"I see I arrived just in time," _Aanlahaash_ said, as he laid several clusters of the _kóox_ down before them. "It's a good thing I came back when I did or I would have missed out entirely."

Aanlahaash grabbed a bowl and scooped out a generous portion of the clam mixture for himself. "Hopefully we can get some game tonight and can make some stew with the _kóox_."

When the group had finished their morning meal they once again boarded the _yaakw_ and paddled out to sea. As they paddled on they came upon a bay (Funter Bay) with semi-open waters and saw some smoke and perhaps even a settlement across the open waters. "I think we are far enough away that those people will not feel threatened by us. We will just keep moving north," Raven's Breath answered the unspoken question on the face of his nephews. So they continued north on their journey to a new land.

The water was rough in the semi-open waters of the bay and the group had to paddle hard to stay above the waves. It could be that the storm the _kaa sháade háni_ at the warm springs mentioned was trying to catch them. The weather however, though breezy, never got too serious.

It was a couple of days later that they came upon Auke _Aan_ (Auke Village) just outside of present-day Juneau, Alaska. The Auke _Kwaan_ (people of Auke) were friendly with them and they enjoyed their visit, but at the end of the second day Raven's Breath announced their intention to move on in the morning.

"We really must keep moving if we are to get settled in a new place before _táakw_ (winter) sets in. We will have to build a house and put up enough salmon, berries, and meat to last until _taakw eetí._

The group set off with well wishes from the Auke _Kwaan_. They continued up the waterways that separated the islands from the mainland in the area that makes up the great archipelago of southeast Alaska and came to the channel known today as Lynn Canal. The air had more of a nip in it than back in _Taan_ - the island home they had left so many days ago. The group felt eager as they entered what seemed to be an unclaimed land. They stopped for the night on a small island (now known as Sullivan Island south of present-day Haines, Alaska). It was lush with fine timbers and easy access to the sea, but Raven's Breath was not satisfied.

"There is too much exposure to the wind," he said, scratching his chin thoughtfully. "We won't want to struggle to keep warm this _táakw_ with that wind to contend with all the time. Let's just keep moving onward." They paddled to the east side of the peninsula and stopped in at a nice cove that seemed to light up with the _kukalt'éex' ká gagaan._

Photo by Ron Horn

"Let's stop here and see what this place has to offer," Raven's Breath instructed his nephews. "Raven's Wing, you take *Skooyéil* with you and scout that area over there," gesturing toward the *shaa* (mountain) people now call Mt. Ripinski but was always referred to as *Géisan* by the Tlingits. "*Aanlahaash*, you and *Kakáayi* go west and see what lies in that direction," Raven's Breath pointed to the area now known as the Chilkat Valley. "I will explore along the shoreline a bit. We will meet back here at the *yaakw* by the time the *gagaan* goes down. *Xat xeeya. áxch agé*?" (Do you understand me?)

"*Aaa*," the nephews spoke as one, then they all set off in different directions.

By evening the group gathered once again to report on what they found. Raven's Wing and *Skooyéil* reported seeing squirrels in the woods, a few rabbits, and some *tsaa* out on the water. Raven's Breath reported that he saw no sign of *guwakaan* (deer) or other wild game along the beach. The group looked at *Aanlahaash* and *Kakáayi* to see what they had to report.

"*Káak*, we found a big *héen* (river) on the other side there," *Aanlahaash* pointed west.

"*Aaa*, and there are a lot of *xáat* in the *héen*," *Kakáayi* gushed, his eyes twinkling with excitement. Just then he pulled out two *xáat* (salmon), one large *T'á* (King Salmon), and a *Gaat* (Sockeye) he had hid behind a log just before they got to the beach. The others cheered. "Ho-ho-ho-ho," Raven's Wing laughed and slapped Aanlahaash on the shoulder and *Kakáayi* on the back.

"*Éi---tsk* (the best)," Raven's Breath said as held the two *xáat* up in the air to get a better look.

"The river is just teeming with x̱áat," Aanlahaash said. He brought his hands forward and made an agitating movement with them so the crew could get the full picture.

"You've convinced me," Raven's Breath said. "Tomorrow morning let's pull the yaakw up into that tall grass so it will not be easily seen. Then let's pack all our things over to the héen, and then come back for the yaakw. We will carry it on our shoulders over to the héen so we don't have to paddle back around."

The next morning, the nephews wasted no time in carrying out their uncle's command. Aanlahaash and Ḵaḵáayi led the way and the others followed.

"It is really not that far. We just need to get to the top of this hill and then it levels off. We should be there well before midday," Aanlahaash said.

They walked through the brush mixed with alder, willow, dúḵ (cottonwood), and a few maple, red osier dogwood, and plenty of k'inchéiyi (wild roses). As they approached the héen there were some marshy areas that had purple irises and much skunk cabbage. When they arrived at the héen's edge they indeed saw a lot of action in the water as the x̱áat made their way upriver.

Photo by Ron Horn

"It certainly does look promising," Raven's Breath said excitedly. "Let's hurry back and get the *yaakw*. I want to see what is upriver." The group retraced their steps back to the beach where their *yaakw* waited. When they arrived they found it exactly as they left it--- further proof of no human habitation in the area.

"I think if we find some long poles we can carry the *yaakw* easier," Raven's Breath suggested.

They found two long driftwood poles and cut them to length with an ax-like tool made of beaver's tooth lashed with leather to a wooden handle. Soon they were able to position the *yaakw* onto the poles, upside down. They had cushioned the contact points with some folded pieces of deer hide. When all was ready the four nephews lifted the poles with the *yaakw* and began to move. Their legs took short steps at first as they tried to get in stride with one another. *Skooyéil* began singing the canoe song once again and that seemed to help. They made their way through the brush and marsh once again and before they knew it they were on the bank of the *héen*. Upon their arrival they set the *yaakw* down next to the *héen*. The x̱áat were still active around them as they set the *yaakw* in. Raven's Breath held the handmade rope to keep the *yaakw* from drifting away as they loaded it. When everything was loaded, *Aanlahaash* said he could hold the *yaakw* while the others boarded. After the others boarded, *Aanlahaash* heaved the *yaakw* off the sandy bank and jumped on board himself. The group pulled hard on their paddles but the *héen's* current was strong in spite of its languid appearance so they moved slowly.

"Pull over," Raven's Breath commanded. "I have an idea."

The nephews did as he asked. More than likely they were quite relieved that he might have a better way. They watched as their *káak* lashed one of the driftwood poles to the seat in the middle of the yaakw. He brought out a cedar bark mat that was quite large, about the length of a man and a half, and equally as wide. Raven's Breath charged *Ḵakáayi* to cut two *asyádi* (saplings) which he then lashed to the top and bottom of the cedar bark mat. Raven's Breath lashed the mat, *asyádi* and all to the driftwood pole in the center of the *yaakw*.

Immediately it caught the breeze that was blowing from the southeast and began pushing them upriver.

"Ho-ho-ho, *Káak*. Aren't you are a clever one for thinking of that!" *Aanlahaash* shouted as they once again set off.

This time, with the help of the wind, the travelers made much better time. By evening they had made it about six miles upriver. They pulled up by a rushing freshwater stream and waterfall. The water was cold and refreshing. They all drank and bathed in it as if

Photos by Ron Horn

they were preparing for something special. While Raven's Breath made a x'aan, Kakáayi took his gaffing pole down and speared a xáat. He gutted it, rinsed it off in the stream and brought to the x'aan where Raven's Breath had already started heating rocks to put into their wooden cooking pot. The pot was filled with water and Skooyéil found some Yaana.éit (cow parsnip) growing in a shady spot next to the héen. He added the yaana.éit to the útxli to give a little different flavor. The group settled down for the evening. The cottonwood leaves rustled in the breeze and a slight scent of the sea still hung in the air even though they were miles from salt water.

"I think this is a pretty good place. It is still a little windy here, though. I think it would be better to keep moving upstream, at least to check it out," Raven's Breath said. His eyes had a far-off look to them, as if he was seeing what the future held. "If what we find isn't as good as this we can come back here."

"I would be pleased to stay here," *Kakáayi* interjected. "The *xáat* are certainly plentiful here."

"Well, you know the *xáat* swim upstream. They are probably just as plentiful further on. Besides, we can only eat so much *xáat*. We wouldn't want to be disrespectful and take more than we need," Raven's Breath admonished. The group continued to talk about what might lie ahead of them until late into the evening. Finally, when it got too dark and the *x'aan* had died down to just some glowing embers, they drifted off to sleep. During the night they woke to the sound of a nasal roar. A *xóots* had found their cooking pot with the remaining *útxli*. The group had carelessly left the wooden pot half filled with liquid and the *xáat* remains.

"Copy me," whispered Raven's Breath as he slowly backed away from the hairy beast. The others followed. They retreated to the *héen* and hopped into their *yaakw* just in case the *xóots* had followed them. The *xóots* did not follow but stayed at their camp and turned all their belongings upside down, apparently looking for more food. Finding none, he disappeared back into the woods toward the mountainside.

Photos by Ron Horn

"*Xwéi* (What a relief)," *Skooyéil* sounded when they could no longer hear the *xóots*.

"That was foolish of us to not take care of the remaining food," Raven's Breath scolded. "We must pay closer attention to what we do from here on out. We only have each other to depend upon, and we don't want to lose anyone because of carelessness." The group was thoroughly awake and though the *gagaan* did not show itself it was starting to get fairly light.

"We might as well get moving. We are certainly not going to get any more sleep now. Pack up your things and put them on the *yaakw*. We are leaving." Raven's Breath looked at his nephews who were sitting passively in the *yaakw*. "*Yeedát*! (Now!)" Raven's Breath roared. The nephews jumped, startled at the way their *káak* raised his voice at them. He was not one to easily lose his temper. Still stunned, they moved quickly and quietly, afraid to anger their *káak* any further.

For most of the morning the atmosphere was tense due to Raven's Breath's angry outburst. By the middle of the day, however, the easy atmosphere was restored when Raven's Breath shared a humorous story from his youth. He knew it was just as much his fault as theirs that the pot of *útxli* was left out all night and he had no call to yell at them like that. Fear had ignited his temper. He would never forgive himself, nor would his sisters forgive him, if he let anything happen to his nephews. They were all he had. They were loyal to him and he had to let them know he appreciated them for being there with him. The story he told revealed his ignorance as a youth and the retelling of his *káak's* shortness with him made his nephews realize that their káak was just like them in his youth.

About 10 miles upriver, as we count distance today, the group again pulled up to take a short rest. They lingered in a slough where they thought they might see some <u>x</u>áat swimming into the clear, shallow water.

Photo by Ron Horn

"This might be a good place to settle," Raven's Breath thought out loud.

"Still seems kind of windy to me," *Aanlahaash* replied. "Remember, *Káak*, you didn't want to stay downriver because of the wind," *Aanlahaash* reminded him gently.

"You are right. The wind helps us move upriver but I wouldn't want to put up with it during *táakw*. Something tells me it could be pretty miserable during *táakw* when that wind will be mixed with the snow," Raven's Breath said. They stayed briefly before moving on. The wind was blowing steadily so they made good time. By nightfall they had traveled another five miles. They stayed on a small island in the river and slept peacefully through the night. No night visitors there.

The next morning they ate a light breakfast of dried *cháatl* and cold water. No *x'aan* was lit as they were eager to get going. They propped up their makeshift sail and began their journey once again. The wind was intermittent so their progress was slowed. The toil of paddling upriver did not dampen their enthusiasm, however, as there was a keen sense of anticipation. It was as if they knew they were nearing their final destination. By the time *gagaan* was at its highest point they had reached what is now the 19-mile slide area, but at that time there was no indication of any recent avalanches. The group pulled up on the riverbank and Raven's Breath looked around.

"*Aaah*, this looks good. Let's have a look around and see what we can find out about this place," Raven's Breath said as he hopped out of the *yaakw*.

Once again he instructed his nephews to scout the area and report back by nightfall. The nephews paired off again, *Aanlahaash* and *Kakáayi*, sons of Raven's Breath's elder sister, and *Skooyéil* and Raven's Wing, sons of his younger sister. Raven's Breath joined in scouting. He thought he saw a few *gooch* (wolves) across the river, but before he could get a good look they disappeared into some brush. He saw some sign of either a seek (black bear) or *xóots* when he was walking. There were definitely bear trails through the area.

There must be a den somewhere up this mountainside, Raven's Breath thought to himself. I best not stray too far from the *yaakw* while I am on my own here. He walked a little further and then turned back toward the *héen*. He sat and waited by the *yaakw*. At the close of the day *Skooyéil* and Raven's Wing returned and just when the sky was beginning to darken and Raven's Breath began to worry about *Aanlahaash* and *Kakáayi*, they came back and were exuberant.

Photo by Lani Hotch

"We found a good place, *Káak*," *Aanlahaash* blurted. "There is no wind, and there is a nice little spring that comes right out of the rocks in the mountain, I followed it up to that point," he said, gesturing in a westerly direction. "The water is clear, and *linúkts*. Best I ever had. We saw porcupines, *jánwu* (mountain goat), *xóots*, and of course all the *xáat* we could ever want. We won't have to go far for our food, just like you were hoping for. You have got to see it. It is just a little farther upriver. *Káak*, you must come and see it."

Photos by Ron Horn

"Okay, nephew. You have convinced me once again. We will go first thing in the morning." It was hard for the group to get to sleep that night. They were all so excited about the place *Aanlahaash* and *K̲akáayi* found. It seemed they had just got to sleep when they heard *Aanlahaash* rustling up a *x'aan* in the early morning light.

"*Haa-íh* (You've got to be kidding), brother," *K̲akáayi* said. "We've only just got to sleep and now you're already up fixing *x'aan*."

"Well, it won't take us that long to get there, brother, and then you can sleep again if you want to. I want our *káak* to see what a great place we found. I know he is going to like it."

The conversation of *Aanlahaash* and *K̲akáayi* woke the others and soon they were all sitting around the *x'aan* sipping tea from their wooden bowls.

"I don't see any sign of people living here. I have a good feeling this may be the place if it is as good as you nephews make it sound," Raven's Breath said, stroking his chin thoughtfully. "There seem to be a lot of good trees for building, too. We will want to get started on a house right away. *Táakw* will be here before we know it. It may come a lot sooner than it did on *Taan* as we have come quite a ways north. Not to mention that we have come a good distance inland, too. The air will not be warmed by the ocean as it happens on *Taan*. Perhaps that will mean less rain, though," Raven's Breath concluded.

"I say let's stop talking and go see this land of dreams," Raven's Wing said as he threw the last few drops of tea on the *x'aan*.

"Yes, let's get going," *K̲akáayi* agreed. "I'm awake now, might just as well be on our way." *K̲akáayi* downed the last of his tea and stood up to stretch. They put out the *x'aan* and began to load their things back onto the yaakw for what they hoped would be the last leg of their journey.

The daylight was increasing but *g̲ag̲aan* had not risen above the *shaa* yet. The *dúk̲* (cottonwoods), still newly budded, scented the cool morning air. They paddled quietly though there was little wind to help them. The sail was of little use now. Raven's Breath had cut a long pole that he used to shove into the *héen* bottom to push them along while his nephews paddled. They continued on like this for most of the morning and when they came around a bend in the *héen*, *Aanlahaash* pointed to where a stream entered it.

"*Wéi du*, *Wéi du* (Over there, over there)," he said excitedly, pointing to where a clear, sparkling stream entered the *héen*. "Let's pull over right there." The group paddled quickly to where the mouth of the stream was and pulled their *yaakw* onto a bar of sand. They all leaped out and the first thing that Raven's Breath did was to scoop up some water from the clear cold stream with his hand and taste it.

"*Linúkts*," he said, smiling big. "You were right, *linúkts*."

"Look toward the top of the mountain, *Káak*. See that slope just above the tree line? *Jánwu*! Do you see them? Those white dots on that slope. Lots of them! With all the x̱áat, the *jánwu*, *xóots*, and even porcupine, we won't ever go hungry."

Photos by Ron Horn

Aanlahaash was so excited his words flowed like white water over rapids. His excitement was contagious. The other nephews and Raven's Breath began exploring the area. There were *kaxwéix* (highbush cranberries), plenty of *k'inchéiyi*, ferns, *yaana.éit* and other edible plants. There was a good variety of trees and shrubs, though *dúk* seemed to be the most prevalent.

"I think this will suit us just fine," Raven's Breath said to himself and then he called all his nephews to come and join him near the river's edge. "*Haa-haa-haa-haa-haa,*" he said loudly, pounding a walking stick on the ground. "*Haa-haa-haa-haa-haa,*" he repeated. This was a signal to his nephews that he had something very important to say. They all stood at attention waiting for what was to come. Raven's Breath bent down and scooped up some of the sand and gravel at his feet.

"*Haa aani áyá* (This is our land)," Raven's Breath announced. He looked at his four nephews and locked eyes with each one of them in turn. "Now you say it." The nephews did as they were told. "*HAA AANI ÁYÁ,*" they said together. Then Raven's Breath bent down again and scooped up some water where the stream mingled with the héen and said, "*Haa héeni áyá* (This is our water)." The nephews followed suit. "*HAA HÉENI ÁYÁ,*" they repeated. Then the nephews broke into a spontaneous round of cheers. *Aanlahaash* and *Kakáayi* did a little victory dance and their cousins and *Káak* joined in as they all celebrated their arrival to, and possession of, their new home.

"Now the work begins," Raven's Breath said under his breath when they finished their little celebration. "Now the work begins."

Photo by Ron Horn

Lani Hotch is a Klukwan resident who lives a traditional subsistence lifestyle, putting up traditional foods such as salmon, berries, wild game, and foods grown from her garden. Lani was born in Klukwan and has lived there most of her life. She and her husband, Jones Hotch, Jr., whose Tlingit name is *Naatl'*, have been married for over 30 years at the time of this writing (2012) and have three grown children. Creating traditional textile arts such as Chilkat and Ravenstail weaving and felt appliqué button blankets are a passion with Lani. She has woven six major pieces herself thus far, and has taken the lead on three group weaving projects.

Ms. Hotch was also instrumental in developing the Klukwan Traditional Knowledge Camp — providing grant writing and administrative support to the building projects as well as coordinating the activities of the camp.

Writing is not Lani's first love but she has written this series of books out of a desire to share this important history with the generations to come. Lani is a member of the *Kaagwaantaan* clan, Wolf House (*Gooch Hít*) and Eagle (*Ch'áak'*) moiety in Klukwan.

Glossary

Aaa - yes

Aaa, yéi nateech - Yes, it doesn't get any better than this

aaah, linúkts, káak - it tastes sweet uncle

Adoo sa wéi idakatyeeháan - Who are all of you?

asyádi - saplings

atx'aan hídi - smokehouse

at x'éeshi - dried fish

Auke Aan - Auke Village

Auke Kwaan - people of Auke

ax eet yaan uwahaa, kunax - I am very hungry

cháatl - halibut

dís - moon

dúk - cottonwood

Gaanaxtéidi - Klukwan Raven Clan

gaat - sockeye

gagaan - sun

gooch - wolves

gook dei - let's go

Gunalcheesh kunax - thank you very much

guwakaan - deer

haa aani áyá - this is our land

haa héeni áyá - this is our water

Haa Shagéinya - Our Creator

haa-íh - you've got to be kidding

héen - river

jánwu - mountain goat

k̲aa sháade háni - clan leader/ spokesperson

k'áach' - red ribbon seaweed

Kaagwaantaan - Eagle Clan

káak - maternal uncle

káani - brother-in-law

kanat'á - blueberries

kaxeéix - highbush cranberries

kéidladi - seagull

k'inchéiyi - wild roses

kóox - chocolate lily/rice

laak̲'ásk - black seaweed

léelkw - grandparents

linúkts - sweet

shaa - mountain

sháal - fish trap

seek - black bear

s'ikshaldéen - Labrador tea

T'á - king salmon

táakw - winter

taakw eetí - spring

taan goo dax - we come from sealion

tláak'w - maternal aunt

tláa - mother

tsaa - harbor seal

tsaa eex̲ - seal oil

Glossary continued

útxli - boiled fish

wéi du - over there

x'aan – fire

xáat - salmon

xat xeeya. áxch agé? - do you understand me?

xóots - brown bear

xwéi - what a relief

yaakw - canoe

yaana.éit - cow parsnip

yáay - whale

yakéi - that's good

yeedát! - now!

Yee sikóo gé? - Do you all know it?

yei awé - that's right

yéil - raven

Yéilkaa - Raven Man

Yen gé yeewunéi idakatyeehan? - are you all ready?

Made in the USA
Lexington, KY
22 February 2018